The Anxiety Workbook for Teens:

The Complete Guide to Help Teens and Young Adults Boost Their Confidence and Self-Esteem (Overcome Worry, Stress, Depression, Shyness, and Fear)

Rachel Stone

© Copyright 2018 by Rachel Stone - All rights reserved.

The following Book is reproduced below with the goal of providing information that is as accurate and reliable as possible. Regardless, purchasing this eBook can be seen as consent to the fact that both the publisher and the author of this book are in no way experts on the topics discussed within and that any recommendations or suggestions that are made herein are for informational purposes only. Professionals should be consulted as needed prior to undertaking any of the action endorsed herein.

This declaration is deemed fair and valid by both the American Bar Association and the Committee of Publishers Association and is legally binding throughout the United States.

Furthermore, the transmission, duplication, or reproduction of any of the following work including specific information will be considered an illegal act irrespective of if it is done electronically or in print. This extends to creating a secondary or tertiary copy of the work or a recorded copy and is only allowed with an express written consent from the Publisher. All additional rights reserved.

The information in the following pages is broadly considered a truthful and accurate account of facts. As such, any inattention, use, or misuse of the information in question by the reader will render any resulting actions solely under their purview. There are no scenarios in which the publisher or the original author of this work can be in any fashion deemed liable for any hardship or damages that may befall them after undertaking information described herein.

Additionally, the information in the following pages is intended only for informational purposes and should thus be thought of as universal. As befitting its nature, it is presented without assurance regarding its prolonged validity or interim quality. Trademarks that are mentioned are done without written consent and can in no way be considered an endorsement from the trademark holder.

Table of Contents

Introduction
Chapter 1: Understanding Worry and Anxiety
    Panic Attacks
    Social Anxiety
        Overcoming Social Anxiety
        Social Anxiety Challenges
Chapter 2: Overcoming Your Shyness
Chapter 3: Improving Self-Perception
    Worksheets
        My Perception of My Strengths and Weaknesses
        My Best Friend's Perception of My Strengths & Weaknesses
        My Parent's Perception of My Strengths & Weaknesses
        My _____ Perception of My Strengths & Weaknesses
    Self-Perception and Self-Esteem
Chapter 4: Stressors and Anti-Stress Practices
    Causes of Stress
    Anti-Stress Practices
Chapter 5: Courage Conquers Fear
    Managing Fear
    Managing Phobias
    Worksheets to Guide You through Analyzing, Managing, and Overcoming Phobias
        Identifying My Phobia
        Conquering My Phobia
Chapter 6: Battling Depression
    What Causes Depression?
    Sadness Vs. Depression

    Do I Have Depression
  Managing Depression
Chapter 7: Self-Confidence Revolution
  Self -Empowerment
    Techniques for Self-Empowerment
  Positive Affirmation
    Examples of Affirmations
  Setting Goals
    Daily Goals
    Short-Term Goals
    Long-Term Goals
Conclusion
Resources
References
Our Other Book

Introduction

Congratulations on purchasing *The Anxiety Workbook for Teens: The Complete Guide to Help Teens and Young Adults Boost Their Confidence and Self-Esteem (Overcome Worry, Stress, Depression, Shyness, and Fear)* and thank you for doing so.

The following chapters will discuss how to deal with the difficulties of being a teen and a young adult in today's society. It seems like overnight that we go from playing hide-and-seek to being faced with peer pressure to play drinking games. Suddenly, we are expected to know what we want to do with our lives, and it seems like every decision could affect the rest of our lives. Compound that with changing bodies, mercurial friendships, the sudden desire for romantic relationships, and the growing importance of popularity, which is fleeting and often based on things out of our control. No wonder teens become anxious!

This book will remind you that everything you are feeling is normal, and it will help you find ways to deal with stress, anxiety, depression, shyness, and fear. You will be given practical suggestions for exercises and practices to help make you a happier, healthier, and more productive person during your teen and young adult years and beyond. The social and coping tools you develop now will help you in the future. You will be reminded throughout this book that you are normal, the way you feel is normal, you are a worthwhile person, and making mistakes will not negate this. All that is asked of you is that you try to make yourself as happy, healthy, and successful as you can and want to be.

I hope that you find this book to be an approachable guide to being your best, anxiety-free, and brave self. If you find it helpful or interesting, please leave a review on Amazon!

There are plenty of books on this subject on the market, thanks again for choosing this one! Every effort was made to ensure it is full of as much useful information as possible, please enjoy!

Chapter 1: Understanding Worry and Anxiety

For many of us, the teenage years are when we really start to experience stress in our lives. We start making important decisions on our own, instead of having them made for us by authority figures. *Should I go to that concert instead of studying for the final? Should I post that risqué Snapchat photo? Should I sneak out in the middle of the night and meet my boyfriend/girlfriend? Where do I want to go to college? Do I even want to go to college? What do I major in?* Although stress is normal, for many people, it can develop into real anxiety.

External pressures are the most obvious source of stress and anxiety for teens and young adults. School gets serious. High school grades affect where we get into college. College classes affect what direction our careers will take. For others, sports have similar stressors. What school will give me a scholarship if I throw this fast, jump this high, or tackle these many people?

Is there a teen movie that doesn't deal with popularity? I don't think there is. All of a sudden, we go from *everybody in the class gets invited to every party* to *you can't sit with us* at lunch. Popularity is often based on aspects of a person outside of their control: how much money their family has and what kind of car they (or their parents or guardian) drive, sexual experience, athletic talent, skills, and looks. It can also be much more fleeting and intangible than that. It's important to remember that popularity doesn't actually mean people like you (as referred to any teen movies ever made).

Internal pressures are less easy to define. *Am I good enough? Am I pretty enough? Am I masculine enough? Is the way I'm feeling about my sexuality normal? What will I do with my life?* I'll tell you a secret: these fears don't go away, although they change. You may worry about being a good son or daughter, but I guarantee that your parents or guardian are even more worried about being a good mother, father, or guardian.

It is important to learn how to deal with your anxiety. It is easy to let it slip into negative behaviors, but in the long run, facing your anxiety head-on will make you a happier and healthier person. Negative behaviors can become a vicious cycle. If you decide to skip school, or just a class, because you are nervous about speaking or answering questions, this just leads you to be further behind. The teen and young adult years are when many people are first exposed to alcohol and other illegal substances. If abused, this can easily become a crutch people use to escape their stress and anxiety. This can have serious short-term and long-term repercussions.

The short-term effect can be expulsion from school, cut from sports teams, arrested for underage drinking, or just do something foolish in front of your peers, therefore increasing your anxiety. The long-term effect can be addiction and other serious diseases.

Panic Attacks

Anxiety, if left unchecked, can develop into panic attacks. Panic attacks can develop suddenly and have a myriad of symptoms. The most common symptoms are shortened breaths, dizziness, nausea, and a rapid heartbeat. If you have a panic attack, you are not being overdramatic. It is your body's involuntary way of reacting to your emotional and mental state.

Panic attacks are very uncomfortable and can be quite scary. The first thing you need to do is admit to yourself you are having a panic attack. It is not anything to be ashamed of, and you're not going to die—remind yourself of these things. Think yourself a mantra of *"I'm going to be OK. It is just a panic attack."* Keep repeating this to yourself. Say it out loud if that helps you, and is appropriate to the situation (i.e. not in the middle of a class). Do not let yourself go into a mental spiral of fear about what is happening to you. Breathe deeply and slowly. Some people even recommend holding your breath for short intervals. If you are in a stressful environment, shut your eyes and block out the stressful stimuli. If your environment is not stressful, put all your focus on something that calms you. This could be anything: a picture, a childhood toy, or a person. Try to think about something positive, as people say, go to your "happy place."

Tell your friends and family what is helpful to you when you experience panic attacks. Make sure they know that telling you to calm down is quite unlikely to be helpful!

Do you want space? Do you want a hug? A hot mug of chamomile tea, or a cold glass of water? Silence or music? Whatever puts you at ease. We will discuss ways to deal with anxiety, which should help prevent panic attacks. However, if you experience them with regularity, or in situations where it puts you or the people around you at risk (such as when you are driving), you should talk to your doctor.

Social Anxiety

During teen years, many people develop social anxiety, which is experienced as the fear of judgment in social or public situations. This can be experienced as nervousness before anything from giving an oral report in school, going to a party, to deciding where to sit in the cafeteria. This can certainly have its benefits. If you're nervous about that report, you are more likely to practice and rehearse; however, it can have its downside. Teens and young adults and people of all ages, with advanced social anxiety, will tend to avoid certain social situation altogether. This can lead to feeling left out and depressed, which can make social anxiety even worse when the next social situation arises.

Do you have social anxiety? Check the following statements if they apply to you:

☐ I often avoid social situations because I feel I'm being judged by my peers.

☐ I have physical symptoms of my nervousness in social situations (blushing, rashes, stuttering, shaking).

☐ I have physical symptoms of my nervousness in social situations AND THAT MAKES IT SO MUCH WORSE!

- [ ] My anxiety regularly affects my home life, schoolwork, friendships, and romantic relationships.

- [ ] I dread one-on-one conversations with people I'm not close to.

- [ ] I seldom feel comfortable in a group of strangers.

- [ ] I frequently use my phone as a buffer when I feel uncomfortable talking to people (not just because I want to post an update).

If you have checked three or more of these, you likely have social anxiety. But don't lose hope! Identifying the issue is the first step in improving it.

Overcoming Social Anxiety

Let yourself imagine the worst possible outcome of the situation. Then, consider the likelihood that this will occur. Let's say French is your worst class, and you have an oral report. Your worst-case scenario could be that you get up to the front of the class, open your mouth to begin, vomit all over the podium, and be expelled. But, this is your life, not a movie, and that is NOT going to happen. The likely outcome is that you will stumble over a few words, blush a little, and get through the report just fine. Do you care if someone blushes during a report? Probably not. Are most people even going to be paying attention to you? Probably not.

Sure, you may have to look at your notes more than you'd like, but that's okay!

There's a party on Friday night that you're nervous about. What's the worst-case scenario? Everyone will point and laugh when you show up and refuse to let you in? You'll walk around with toilet paper on your shoes and have to change schools? Guess what. It's still your life, not a movie; that's not going to happen. Other people are insecure too! They are too busy worrying about how they are being judged to judge you. If you end up being a wallflower, that is perfectly fine. Look for another wallflower and try to bond. They will be grateful! If someone laughs at you, it will be more likely that you said something funny. But, just in case, always check your shoes and pants for toilet paper when leaving the bathroom. Words to live by.

Use that nervous energy to prepare. Nerves can be a good thing! If we didn't sense danger, mankind would have died out thousands of years ago. Harness that energy. Our ancestors did so by sheltering themselves from the elements and fleeing or hiding from predators. You can still use those instincts.

If you are feeling nervous about that French report, practice it! Stand in front of the mirror, and give yourself the report. You will likely feel awkward and silly. Good! Get those feelings out now! Practice as much as you can, and muscle memory will help you get through the report.

Before that party you're scared to go to, do something that makes you feel confident and good about yourself.

Go for a run. Lift some weights. Paint your nails. Wear your favorite perfume or cologne. Listen to your favorite music. Play the guitar. Get ready with a friend. Whatever makes you feel good about you! Plan some things to talk about. You can even jot them down, so you remember them better (whatever you do, do NOT bring these notes with you, and password-protect your phone!). Get yourself into a positive mental place, in which you are feeling confident before you even enter into the situation. It will carry over.

Change the way you think by changing the way you talk. The easiest person to criticize is yourself. Stop! It's easier said than done. But, here is the secret: the first step is to stop verbalizing it. Instead of saying, "*This dress makes me look fat*" say "*This dress doesn't fit well.*" Instead of saying, "*I suck at playing guitar*" say "*I want to take guitar lessons.*" When you get in the habit of not saying these things, it gets increasingly easier not to think them. If you find yourself dwelling on the negatives about yourself, do something to distract yourself. Read. Take a walk. Play a game on your phone. Talk to friends. Listen to music. Do something to occupy your mind with something other than what you perceive as your faults. Once you have cleared your mind, so you are no longer dwelling on the negatives, logically assess what you were thinking about. Were you being overly critical of yourself about something you cannot help? Was it something that you can work on improving to better yourself and your life? Once you have pinpointed what you want to improve, you are ready for the next step.

Take action. Are you struggling in a particular subject in school? Talk to your teacher or professor and ask for advice. Do they think you would benefit from a tutor? Do they recommend a tutor? Maybe they will even offer to work with you after school a couple of days a week. Are you the new kid at school? Start joining clubs, sports, and activities that will help you to get to know people with similar interests quickly. Are you nervous to talk to people because you're a "theatre geek"? GOOD! Join the drama club. Are you a nerd who is more at home in the science lab than a party? GOOD! Join the STEM club. Are you self-conscious because you aren't great in school, but love fashion? GOOD! Do costumes for the drama club. Do you love sports but aren't coordinated? GOOD! Join the track team. Are you tall and awkward? GOOD! Try out for basketball. Do you prefer to reading to talking to people? GOOD! You can join a book club.

Final thoughts on anxiety: You are not the only one. Plenty of adults deal with it too. Having anxiety doesn't make you weird or crazy. It is a normal and common reaction to the stressors in your life. If you need help, ask for it. Family members, friends, teammates, guidance counselors, teachers, coaches, etc. will help you. If anyone judges you, that is not a reflection on you; it is a reflection on them. It is OK to ask for help. There are even apps that help you with stress management. If working through things on your own and with the important people in your life is not enough, it's OK to get therapy. If you, your parent(s) or guardian, and doctor all agree that you would benefit from anti-anxiety medication, please remember that this is nothing to be ashamed of. Starting and stopping medications should only be done under advisement and supervision of a medical professional.

Social Anxiety Challenges

Check off once complete. Do as many or as few as you like. Make your own, based on situations that make you nervous, that you particular areas you want to improve on.

- [ ] Participate in a class discussion in your best class.

- [ ] Participate in a class discussion in your worst class.

- [ ] Strike up a conversation with someone at school to whom you've never spoken.

- [ ] Strike up a conversation with a stranger (in a safe and public setting).

- [ ] Sit and have a coffee by yourself at a cafe, without being on your phone the whole time.

- [ ] Show up at a party by yourself.

- [ ] Try out for a sport.

- [ ] Join a club.

- [ ] Offer to show the new kid around school.

☐ Take a walk. Look up, not at your phone or the ground. Acknowledge people you pass (smile, say "*Hi*", wave).

☐ _____

☐ _____

☐ _____

☐ _____

☐ _____

☐ _____

☐ _____

☐ _____

☐ _____

☐ _____

☐ _____

☐ _____

Chapter 2: Overcoming Your Shyness

Being shy is a personality trait like any other. It can be innate or develop over time. Approximately 20% of Americans are born shy[1], while 40% of American adults report that they are shy. This additional 20% can be attributed to learned behaviors, life experiences, or the result of low self-esteem. Shyness has a bad reputation but is not a bad quality. However, it can make life more difficult, and other people tend to misinterpret shyness. Being shy and being an introvert are not mutually inclusive. Introverts crave time alone, as this is how they relax and recharge. This does not mean they are not comfortable in social situations; they just need time alone as well. Shyness is feeling awkward or unduly nervous around other people, and shy people can often feel self-conscious as a result.

Shy people can be perceived by others as snobby or rude. This is simply not true, but the perception affects how people treat the shy person, thus making him or her feel even more self-conscious. People may think that a shy person does not want to be around others. Many shy people are extroverts in hiding. They want to be around people and interact, but they just don't know how to go

---

[1] https://www.psychologytoday.com/us/articles/199511/the-cost-shyness

about doing so. It is challenging for an outgoing person to understand how a shy person feels.

There are varying degrees of shyness. Shy people may have trouble upholding their end of the conversation, have difficulty making eye contact, and go to great lengths to avoid social situations. This type of shyness has outward signs and is quite easy for others to identify. The majority of shy people can fake ease in a social situation, but inside they are analyzing everything they are saying, worrying about how others perceive them, and admonishing themselves for what they see as mistakes. The commonality is that both types are self-conscious, and in a vicious cycle, self-conscious about being perceived as self-conscious!

Shyness can lead to undesired isolation, social anxiety, low self-esteem, fear of rejection, and depression. It can make interviews much more difficult, whether they are for college admissions or a job. Some jobs would be almost impossible for a shy person to succeed in. You may never become an outgoing person, you might always be a little more reserved (which has its own benefits), but you can overcome your shyness.

Start small and practice in comfortable situations. Being shy doesn't mean you don't have friends. Concentrate on displaying more confident behaviors around them. Body language conveys confidence, and this is easy to fake! Straighten your back, push your shoulders down and back, smile, and make eye contact. You can do all these things without even speaking, and it makes a huge difference in how you are perceived. If you usually are fairly quiet in conversations, even with your closest friends, use this as your starting point for participating more.

Practice and rehearse. When in doubt, ask someone a question. Most people love talking about themselves. Memorize some questions and topics to talk about. If your delivery is a little stiff, that's fine. What's important is that you are trying and interacting. Compliments combined with questions are always good conversation starters. For example, you can compliment a football player on their performance in their most recent game and follow that up with a question about when they started playing. This technique works best if you actually mean the compliment!

Stay comfortable. Shy people are constantly worrying about how people are viewing and judging them. If they are particularly nervous, they may start to blush or sweat. Dress in layers. If you are getting nervous, take off a layer before you start to sweat. Its better to be too cold than too sweaty. If you wear makeup, keep it light or use waterproof cosmetics and skip wearing blush. Wear a strong antiperspirant. If you can avoid the physical manifestations, that's one less thing to worry about others noticing. If you blush, remember that cosmetics companies make millions of dollars a year on that lovely flush of color. The next time you feel yourself blushing or sweating, take a look at yourself. It probably feels much worse than it actually is.

Be assertive. Being shy doesn't make you meek. Don't let people take advantage of you. If someone interrupts you while you are speaking, you can politely say, "*Excuse me, can I finish please?*" If you are not ready for that, you can wait until they finish, and pick back up with "*As I was saying,*" and continue on. Assertive does not mean rude. Unfortunately, shy people can sometimes be thought of as rude. Be cognizant of that and counteract it with being as polite as possible. If you are working on a group project and there is an assignment that you are interested in, speak up. You don't have to let others assign you to the worst task.

Stop apologizing all the time. #sorrynotsorry is trending for a reason. Shy people often apologize too much about things they should not be sorry for. Essentially, they are apologizing for their existence. Confident people don't do this. If you accidentally step on someone's foot, by all means, apologize. If you are on time to meet someone but they were early, don't apologize for being late, you're not! If you want to add something to a conversation, don't say, "*I'm sorry, I would just like to add,*" just say, "*I'd like to add,*" and continue on.

Be realistic. Humans are a fairly narcissistic species. As much as you worry about how people perceive you, the person you are talking about is worrying about how you are judging them, or just biding their time until it is their turn to speak. Would you really notice and judge someone for blushing? Likely not, so why would that person notice or care that you were blushing?

Don't label yourself. "*Hi, my name is Kate, and I'm sorry, I'm shy*" is not a good start when you introduce yourself to someone. People see what they expect to see. If you label yourself as shy and share that with people you don't know well, they will see you as a shy person. If you work on acting self-confident, you are more likely to be viewed as a confident, quietly mysterious person. People will wonder what you are thinking, and want to know the answers!

Be yourself. Clichés are often clichés for a reason. You don't have to pretend to be the most confident, talkative person in the room. The goal is to actually feel confident in social situations. Although faking confidence can be very beneficial, don't fake your personality or beliefs. Don't say things just because other people are saying them if you don't agree. Say you don't agree! This can open up a whole new conversation. People won't like you just because you agree with them, but if they notice that you go along with whatever they are saying, they might just start taking advantage of that.

Social anxiety can develop from shyness and can be overcome in similar fashions. The exercises overcoming social anxiety from Chapter 1 will help you get started. Challenge yourself to do something every day that enables you to break out of your shyness. Remember, it is the effort here that really counts. If you tried out for a team but didn't make it, you still have succeeded. You have put yourself in an uncomfortable situation and survived. Join the JV team or try another sport or club.

Chapter 3: Improving Self-Perception

Self-perception deals with the way we view and interpret ourselves and our actions. It is knowing who you are, your strengths, weaknesses, and capabilities. The theory of self-perception is that if we can change the way we behave, it changes how we view ourselves, leading to continued changes in behavior. For a simplistic example, someone feels bad about himself or herself because he or she is out of shape, so he or she starts going for a daily walk. If this person sees and feels a positive change, he or she might start going for a daily jog. Self-confidence can be improved by increasing your knowledge in a particular subject, like practicing a sport or musical instrument, whereas improving your self-perception is more nuanced and subtler. But, don't despair. It can be done!

Get out of the all-or-nothing mindset. You can make a mistake, but that doesn't make you a mistake. If you messed something up, that doesn't mean you will mess everything up. If you cannot do something on the first try, that doesn't mean you can't ever do it. Making a mistake doesn't decrease your self-worth. Instead, use it to identify areas you can work to improve. Referencing our struggling French student from Chapter 1, if you fail a quiz, that doesn't make you a failure. Instead, go over that quiz and figure out your mistakes. Do you have trouble with conjugating verbs or remembering the gender of nouns? Pinpoint the areas you struggle with and use that as your starting point for improvement.

Be honest about your strengths and weaknesses. Many people don't take time to identify their strengths, but they can also be in denial of their weaknesses. Do you think of yourself as a dedicated student because you study for 5 hours a night, but are actually playing on your phone for most of the time? Do you think of yourself as nice to everyone, but tend to gossip behind people's backs? Try writing down 5 to 10 strengths and 5 to 10 weaknesses. Which of your strengths do you want to nurture? Which of your weaknesses do you want to improve upon?

Ask for input. How we view ourselves is often vastly different from how others see us. Pick a couple people you trust, and ask them what they perceive as five of your strengths and five of your weaknesses. You will likely notice a pattern. You will hopefully find strengths you didn't even know about! When you see repeated weaknesses, don't start to spiral into self-doubt and self-recrimination. Instead, use that as a guideline for what to work on first. Your weaknesses are not set in stone. Maybe you have never realized that people perceive you as a gossiper. It's OK! Becoming aware of something is the first step in fixing it. Although tough love can be helpful (stop texting that person who is not responding), be careful whom you ask. If your best friend tends to be overly critical of others, don't ask them. Ask people who genuinely care about you and want the best for you, and will be kind, yet honest.

Make yourself uncomfortable. Take a risk (but don't endanger personal safety)! Although you should be realistic with yourself, you should also be optimistic. If you love English class, and your grade is on the border of whether you should take AP English, sign up for it! If your grades are almost what a college is asking for, apply anyway and wow them with your admittance essay and high SAT and ACT scores. If you like to run, but aren't a sprinter, try out for the cross-country team. If you have a crush on someone, ask them out. If you have a great voice but hesitate to sing in public, try out for the choir. Apply for that dream job in another city. Take a risk and see what you can accomplish. You may just impress yourself. If nothing else, be proud of yourself for trying! You can add *"I'm brave"* and *"I take smart, calculated risks"* to your list of strengths.

Worksheets

My Perception of My Strengths and Weakness

My Best Friend's Perception of My Strengths and Weakness

My Parents' Perception of My Strengths and Weakness

My _____ Perception of My Strengths and Weakness

My Perception of My Strengths and Weaknesses

Strength	Nurture	Weakness	Improve

My Best Friend's Perception of My Strengths & Weaknesses

Strength	Nurture	Weakness	Improve

My Parent's Perception of My Strengths & Weaknesses

Strength	Nurture	Weakness	Improve

My _____
Perception of My Strengths & Weaknesses

Strength	Nurture	Weakness	Improve

Self-Perception and Self-Esteem

Having positive self-perception leads to having better self-esteem. Self-esteem is not thinking you are perfect. It is accepting yourself the way you are while acknowledging and working to improve your weaknesses. It is being proud of yourself for trying to improve. If we want to have a positive relationship with other people, we first need to have a positive relationship with ourselves.

This book discusses trying to think and talk about yourself like you would think and talk to a friend. Be your own friend. Be nice to yourself. Value yourself. Accept your mistakes and know that you can move on from them.

Chapter 4: Stressors and Anti-Stress Practices

Stress has many causes. Many adults wax nostalgic about their teen years, how it was so fun, carefree, stress-free, and idyllic. Well, it might be for some people, but for many others, it's not. In 2014, the American Psychological Association did a survey that found teens and young adults suffered from greater stress than their parents, particularly during the school year. The world is changing. Sports are getting more serious, college admissions more difficult (and expensive), and we cannot escape social media. When your parents were teenagers, if they were being bullied, they got to escape the bullying when they got home from school. With social media, it is impossible to escape. The bullies are in your smartphone and on your computer, texting, PMing/DMing, posting on your wall. Now, you have to worry not just about being judged in face-to-face situations, but also virtually. Do you have enough followers, who are following you (it is best not to accept requests from strangers) and what you're posting?

Causes of Stress

Most teens and young adults will cite school as their number one cause of stress. What classes to take, how many AP classes are too many or too few, if college is right for you, what colleges to apply to, how to pay for it, and what to major in once you get there.

Being a teen is physically difficult! Early bloomers stress about that (Will this ever stop growing?), as well as late bloomers (Will this ever grow?). Our bodies are changing so much, so fast, and there is a huge influx of hormones, so we feel different and confused. Growing pains are real! You can have physical symptoms, such as swollen, painful joints, particularly knees. With all of this strain, teens need much sleep and rarely get enough. Going to bed early is often viewed by peers as "uncool" behavior (but it's not). You are at a time of your life when more sleep is what your body needs. If you need a lot more sleep than the other members of your family, this does not make you lazy. It makes you an average teen.

Social stress is never as difficult as when you are a teen. There is so much pressure to keep up with your peers and to try and be cool. This is always changing. Is it still even cool to use the word "cool'? It's certainly not cool trying to be cool. Is it uncool to use Facebook? Is Snapchat cool enough, or is there a new, cooler app? What designer is cool today that probably won't be cool tomorrow? Who decides these things? The cool kids. How do they get to be cool? Some mysteries will never be solved. However, they have one thing in common: they project confidence! Do they really have it? That is their secret.

Families can be a haven from the world, but they can also add to your stress. Many teens and young adults share in the responsibilities of caring for younger siblings. Most parents or guardians mean well, but they can put much pressure on their child, whether they are living vicariously through them, want them to have a better life, or expect straight A's and a football scholarship. Divorces, remarriages, moves, layoffs, even promotions (that lead to less time at home) affect a teen and young adult. Sibling rivalry is also prevalent. Coaches, parents, guardian, and peers might expect certain things (negative or positive) from someone based on an older sibling.

Do teens ever stop thinking about sex? Romantic relationships are new and scary to a teen. How much attention is too much? How little is too little? There can be peer pressure to go further physically, peer pressure to abstain, and, of course, pressure from partners (a good partner will NOT pressure you). If you decide to have sex, there is the stress of a possible pregnancy and STDs. Whatever you decide to do it, first and foremost, ***respect yourself, your partner, your health, and your partner's health.***

Teens experiencing peer pressure is so prevalent it's almost a cliché. Some peers will pressure you to have sex, and some will insist you should not. Sorority and fraternity members may pressure you to join, and other friends may tell you not to join. Peer pressure tends to have the connotation of participating in negative behaviors. That's not always the truth, but pressure is still pressure. Maybe you are in all honors or AP classes and feel peer pressure to get straight A's. If you do, that is fantastic. If you don't, as long as you've down your best, you should still be proud of yourself.

Teens and young adults are very aware of their appearance. It is a time of huge physical changes. Most people assume that it's mostly something females struggle with, but that is not true. While we won't dive into this subject deeply here, *if anything is preventing you from eating a healthy, well-rounded diet, talk to your parents or guardian, and doctor*. You can also talk to other trusted adults, such as a school nurse, guidance counsellor, or religious leader. The short-term and long-term effects of a not eating enough in general, or overeating a particular food group can be devastating, even deadly.

Anti-Stress Practices

There are as many ways to reduce your stress as there are things to get stressed about. You may find that being alone and quiet works for you, and that's wonderful. You may find that being around other people in an energetic environment works for you, and that's great too. Some people destress on 10-mile runs, others find a nap works better for them. Discovering what works for you is more important than what you actually do. Figuring this out will help you get to know yourself better. You probably already know this, at least subconsciously, but take the time to listen to yourself and your needs.

Practicing meditation and yoga have been used for centuries for many purposes, including stress relief. Take a class, use an app, or do a guided video on YouTube. There are many free options that you can take advantage of, and if you have a gym membership, yoga is a commonly offered class. It takes practice to feel the long-term effects of yoga and meditation. Be patient. There is a reason they are referred to as practices.

Sometimes you need a mental break at school or work. Take some long, slow, deep breaths. Squeeze a stress ball. If you can, take a 5-minute break and walk around. Getting some fresh air and using your leg muscles can help clear your mind.

Laugh yourself towards relaxation. Have you ever truly laughed and felt stressed at the same time? Except for nervous laughter, probably not. When you laugh, it can actually alleviate some of the physical symptoms of stress. It makes you feel more at ease and releases endorphins (a naturally produced hormone that makes you feel happy). Think about when you are in an awkward social situation. Doesn't laughter help break the ice? Watch a funny movie. Spend some time with your funniest friend. Watch silly animal videos on YouTube. Have a joke ready to tell for when you are at a conversational impasse.

You have five senses—use them. This helps to switch your focus from the stressors in your life to what you are experiencing. Look at cute pictures of animals. Put on your favorite perfume, cologne, or light your favorite candle. Listen to your favorite music. If you have a pet, pet it. Have a snack.

Take a mini mental vacation. Spend a few minutes picturing yourself in your favorite serene place. What are you doing while you are there? What can you see, smell, feel, taste, and hear? This can relax both your mind and body, leaving you feeling refreshed when you return to reality.

Escape the pressures of social media, turn off your phone! You can do it. You will survive. Engage in the world around you. Watch a sunset without trying to get the perfect picture. Hang out with your best friend without trying to get the sexiest selfie. Play with your pet without trying to get the cutest video.

Go for a walk or run without listening to music. Listen to the sound of the wind and your breath. Is it spring? Appreciate the blooming flowers. Is it fall? Appreciate the turning leaves. Smell the fresh air. If you are in the city, appreciate the architecture. Pay attention to your body, how it is loosening and warming up, and responding to the activity.

Take a bath. Relax in some Epsom salt and hot water. This relaxes your mind and body. It can ease muscle pains and help you sleep. The Epsom salt will draw toxins out of your body. Don't forget to bring a cold glass of water and some relaxing music or a book.

Mindfully relax your body. When you are in bed, tense up one muscle at a time, then relax it and feel the release. Go through your entire body, one muscle at a time. Focusing on this practice distracts your mind from the stressors in your life, and as a bonus, should help you get to sleep. Stressing about getting to sleep, therefore having a harder time sleeping is so frustrating!

Put it on paper. Journaling can be a fantastic way to reduce stress. Expressing everything you are feeling, everything that is stressing you out to an inanimate object that cannot judge you is very therapeutic. As you write, you may even discover stressors that have been affecting you on a subconscious level. A great time to journal is right before bed. Write it down, acknowledge it, and dismiss it from your mind.

Recognize that dealing with stress with negative behaviors can be both counterproductive and dangerous. Activities such as smoking, drugs, alcohol, skipping school, speeding, hurting oneself or others provide a short-term release. However, they can quickly cause more stress, and can even result in disease and death. It is very important to deal with your stress in prolific ways that make you a happier, healthier, more productive person. Even behaviors such as procrastination, which is not dangerous, is a bad habit to get into and can lead to more stress in your life. Having to finish your math homework while in history class is much more stressful than slogging through those math problems the night before. Cheating during a test would be much more stressful than studying for it. Plagiarizing a paper might be quicker than writing it yourself, but the fear of getting caught is much more stressful, and not to mention the potential consequences to your academic career.

Try several different techniques for relaxation. Pick the ones that feel natural and beneficial for you. Make up your own and experiment with those. Try journaling about this too. Write down how you felt before the technique, how you felt during, immediately after, and the next day.

Chapter 5: Courage Conquers Fear

"Courage is not the absence of fear, but rather the assessment that something else is more important than fear."

Franklin D. Roosevelt (1882-1945)

You are more important than your fears. Your life is more important than your fears. Your friends, family, school, job, hobbies, and pets are more important than your fears.

Fear is a primal instinct that humankind would not have survived without. It is an emotional state with a physical response, known as the fight-or-flight response. Do we flee from what is scaring us or do we challenge it? It is a completely normal, healthy, and often helpful reaction to what or who we perceive as dangerous. Fear can even be fun. Horror movies and haunted houses make their money on adrenaline rushes resulting from fear. Fear keeps us from straying down dark and dangerous alleys. It reminds us to lock our doors and be aware of our surroundings. However, the important thing is to control your fear and not let your fear control you.

Fears can be both instinctual and learned. For example, let's take a ten-year-old boy who lives in the suburbs. We'll call him Eddie. Eddie is on the playground and one day sees a grizzly bear, which he has never seen before, come lumbering over to the swings. He is going to be instinctually afraid. Another day, a thirteen-year-old boy, we'll call him Frank, shows up on the playground. Eddie is not scared of Frank. But, if Frank starts to show up every Wednesday, beats up Eddie, and steals his lunch money, poor little Eddie will learn to fear Frank. If this goes on, he could also develop a fear of kids that look, act, or dress like Frank, as well as fear of Wednesdays and playgrounds.

Fear is one of the basic human emotions, an instinct hardwired into our nervous system. The brain reacts to triggers of fear before we have a chance to analyze and realize that something is dangerous. It puts us on alert. Blood pressure will rise, heartbeats will quicken, breathing will speed up, and it can cause sweating, even in cold temperatures. It may even feel like your senses are heightened.

Fear occurs when a person does not feel safe or secure. Common fears include heights, speaking in public, clowns, and flying. Our fears change as we grow and learn, and as our lives change. A kid that spends half his childhood climbing trees may develop a fear of heights as a teen. This could be because the last time he climbed a tree, he fell and broke his leg or just the knowledge that he could fall and break his leg. Many children fear the dark or being alone. As they grow up, they learn that there are no monsters under the bed and being alone can be relaxing, even invigorating.

Phobias are intense, specific, and irrational fears that hinder a person's life. If you have a phobia, this does not make you an irrational person. This makes you a person with a phobia. You have the choice of whether to try to face and overcome it or let it control your life. You can overcome a phobia. It is not easy, but it is a huge accomplishment.

Managing Fear

The way most people manage fear is avoidance. In some cases, this is good. So, please, continue to avoid creepy alleys and unsteady ladders—fear is reasonable in these cases! Always be aware of your surroundings. When you are walking in a parking lot, look around you. Check in, under, and around your car. Have your keys in your hand before leaving the building. Lock the car doors as soon as you get in. If you have a bad feeling, ask someone to walk with you.

Analyze the situation when you feel the physical symptoms of fear. Are you in actual danger? Is the fight-or-flight response necessary? If you are not actually in danger, acknowledge your fear and start to manage your physical response. Take slow, deep breaths. Try to relax your body. Keep telling yourself you are not in danger. Once you have calmed down, try and figure out exactly what you are afraid of. Once you have pinpointed that, you can start to face and conquer your fears.

Ask questions. Learn all you can about your fear. One fear that many teens and young adults face is their parents or guardians divorcing. If this is something you fear, talk to them. Ask them if their fighting means they are considering a divorce. It could very likely be that fighting is their reaction to stressors in their life outside of their relationship and family and they have not realized that it is affecting you. However, if they admit that divorce is a possibility, discuss it. Get an open dialogue going. Let them know what exactly scares you about the possibility. Ask them what the plan is. Ask them what the custody arrangements would be. Ask them if you would have to move or change schools. Fear of the unknown will drive you to imagine the worst-case scenario. Counteract it by no longer having to guess and imagine.

Do your research. Knowledge can give you power over your fears. If you have a phobia about spiders, look up information on them. Find out what species of spiders live where you do. You will likely find out that most of the spiders in your area are just harmless bugs that eat mosquitos. But, you will also learn what spiders are poisonous, what to look for, and what to do if you are bitten. Fearing a poisonous spider is a smart, rational response. Fearing all spiders can negatively affect your life.

Think about your lifestyle. If you fear clowns but otherwise love the circus, you should work past that fear so you can enjoy the circus. If you are perfectly happy living your life avoiding situations that would involve clowns, move on with your life. Focus on facing fears that actually affect your life.

Managing Phobias

The teen and young adult years are when most people start to face phobias. It is also the best time to start facing them. Phobias, left unchecked, can become lifelong struggles that can seriously impair your life.

Do not blame yourself. There are many causes of phobias. If a parent or guardian or sibling has a phobia, this can be a learned behavior they pass down to you. (***Don't blame them either***, they didn't have this book to help them!) Phobias can also develop as a reaction to a traumatic childhood event. If a dog attacks you, you may develop a phobia of all dogs. If you witness someone drown, you may develop a phobia of water.

Although both sexes can develop phobias, it is more common amongst females than males. If you tend to experience anxiety, you are more prone to develop a phobia. Being told repeatedly to be wary of certain situations can also lead to phobias, even if it is done with the best intentions of keeping you safe.

When you are faced with the object of your phobia, your fear response may cause a panic attack. Please refer to Chapter 1 for advice and strategies to deal with panic attacks. If your phobia is serious enough and hinders your day-to-day life, talk to your parents or guardian about therapy. Hypnosis is a tool frequently used to treat phobias. It allows you to face your phobias from the comfort of a couch under the supervision of a trained professional. After lengthy discussions of the pros and cons and possible side-effects, if you, your parents and guardian, and doctor agree that a minor tranquilizer, antidepressant, or a beta-blocker is a good choice for you, keep in mind, this is normal. You are not crazy or irrational. You are a smart person who is taking charge of your life. Medications should not be started or stopped, unless under the direction or supervision of a doctor.

If your phobia doesn't require the attention of a medical profession, there are many strategies you can use to handle and eventually overcome them. This can also be supplemental to therapy but should not be used in lieu of your doctor's directions. If you chose to tackle your phobia on your own or with the help of your friends and family, you can always change your mind and ask for more help and the insight of a professional.

Desensitize yourself slowly. If you are claustrophobic, do not lock yourself in a tiny closet with the intent to stay there until you are cured. Take small steps to experience your dreaded thing or situation very gradually. If you have a phobia of heights, try to get on the first step of a stepladder and stay there for 30 seconds. Do this every day for a week and try to stay longer. The next week, go up to the second step. Once you get to a height in which a fall could potentially injure you, make sure you have a spotter! If you have a fear of crowds, start spending some more time around groups of people. Start small, then work your way up. When you first begin, stay on the fringes so you can get away easily. If you have a phobia of dogs, start by looking at pictures of puppies online. Watch funny puppy videos. Pet the oldest, gentlest dog you know. You may never want a pet dog, but your life will be more comfortable if you can be around them.

Manage your symptoms. When faced with a phobia, focus on slowing your breaths. This will, in turn, slow your heart rate. If you can do so safely, close your eyes. Relax your muscles. Roll your shoulders to release tension and readjust your posture. Concentrating on your symptoms will also help distract you from the object of your phobia.

Flood your phobia. Some experts praise the technique of flooding the senses with the phobia. A germaphobe could leave the house without their hand sanitizer and spend the day bowling. This technique should be used with caution and common sense. If your phobia is of spiders, you can try to look for some in your yard or pet shop, but do not try to pet a brown recluse spider—they are poisonous. If you have a phobia of dogs, go to a dog park, but don't adopt a dog.

Ask for help. If you are claustrophobic, ask a friend or family member to spend some time riding an elevator with you. They can provide moral support and distraction, even if they don't really understand what you are going through.

Join a support group. Face your fears together. Be reminded that you are not alone. You are not crazy. You are not irrational. It helps to be understood and to know that you will not be judged.

Just do it. If your family has planned a fabulous island vacation, are you going to skip it because you have a flying phobia? I hope not! Prepare yourself with music, magazines, and books. You can use the relaxation techniques from Chapter 4 and go have a great time! Before you go, talk to your family and let them know the best methods for helping and reassuring you. Do some research. Learn how low the statistics are for plane crashes. When they happen, they make the news, but there are thousands of flights every single day without incident. It makes more of an impact to learn it for yourself than to just be told.

Reward yourself for the small steps you take to overcome your phobia. Petting a dog might be an everyday occurrence for many people, but if you have a phobia to dogs, that is a major step for you. If you have a phobia of being in crowds, going to see your favorite band in concert is a huge step. Be proud of yourself! If you are trying a technique and it doesn't work for you, do not get down on yourself. What works for someone will not necessarily work for you. What works for most of the people in your support group might not work for you. Do not give up, just keep trying. Trying is courageous, even if not every single attempt is successful. You can get there eventually.

Worksheets to Guide You through Analyzing, Managing, and Overcoming Phobias

Public speaking is a very common phobia and one that can have a negative impact on your life as a teen, young adult, and beyond. As a teen, it can be very detrimental for certain classes in which you will be expected to speak or give reports. Language classes are common examples. If you have a fear of public speaking, you would have to face that every day and the stress of dreading a class can result in poor performance in other classes. As a young adult, it can be adverse in college acceptances due to low grades in classes where speaking is required and can make college admittance interviews akin to torture.

Similarly, it will make job interviews much more difficult, limit your career opportunities, and prevent future promotions. Although you may always be nervous before public speaking, conquering the fear and quelling the panic are very important to your life. This phobia will be used in an example in the following worksheets. This is a fairly easy phobia to pinpoint. If yours is not, keep going, keep analyzing your physical and emotional reactions to situations. If you have a bad reaction one time, it does not mean you have a phobia. It may just mean you have an oral report due that day and you forgot!

Identifying My Phobia

	Situation	Physical Reaction	Emotional Reaction
ex.	Called on to answer a question in French class. Was unsure but stammered out an answer.	Sweaty palms, heart started racing	Intense nervousness
ex.	Oral report in history. Thought I was well-prepared, couldn't talk, went to nurse.	Panic attack	Terror, embarrassment
1			
2			
3			

	Situation	Physical Reaction	Emotional Reaction
4			
5			
Conclusion		ex. I think I have a phobia of public speaking!	
Conclusion			

Conquering My Phobia

	Technique Used	Situation	Results
ex.	Flooding	Signed to sing by myself at karaoke night.	Hid in the bathroom when my name was called.

	Technique Used	Situation	Results
			Cried.
Thoughts		Flooding is too much for me. I need to start smaller!	
ex.	Ask for help	Went to karaoke night with a bunch of friends and sang as a group.	I stood in the back of the group, but I was still up there, singing!
Thoughts		Keep going. At the next meeting of yearbook club, I'll present my idea for a new section.	
1			
Thoughts			
2			

	Technique Used	Situation	Results
Thoughts			
3			
Thoughts			
4			
Thoughts			
5			
Thoughts			

Chapter 6: Battling Depression

If you suspect you have serious depression and have thoughts of harming yourself or others, or suicidal thoughts, please stop reading this, and tell your parents or guardian, guidance counselor, doctor, or, if you are religious, a leader in your place of worship. You can also call the National Suicide Prevention Hotline, 800.273.8255. While we will discuss how to overcome depression, this book is not a tool equipped to deal with immediate threats to your safety. It is a tool for early diagnostics and prevention. You are not alone. You have many people who love and value you. ***Please value yourself enough to ask for help.***

Some people may tell you that depression does not exist. This is a scientific fallacy. *The goal is for depression not to exist in your life.* There are many different types of depression. During fall and winter months, some people suffer from Seasonal Affective Disorder, which is a temporary form of depression due to lack of sunlight and Vitamin D deficiencies. If you have younger siblings, you may have seen your mother or your female guardian battle postpartum depression. Pregnancy and birth wreak havoc on one's body and hormones, and some women need help to get themselves regulated.

You can choose to be sad. *Depression is not a choice.* It is a physical occurrence in your brain that is preventing your moods from being regulated. Sadness is an emotion. Depression is a medical condition that affects how you feel, act, and think; it has real physical symptoms. A depressed person cannot just cheer up. They may want to, and they can fake it for a few hours, but it doesn't change the way they feel, interpret their experiences, or alter what is happening in their heads. Depression can sometimes last a few months, and then resolve itself, as with Seasonal Affective Disorder.

What Causes Depression?

Although it is not unusual for men to experience depression, it is more commonly found in women. The young adult age group is the most likely to suffer depression. If you experience depression in your lifetime, you are most likely to experience it for the first time in your teenage years. Depression can be genetic. It can occur after a major traumatic event in your life. Some medical conditions and medications can have the side effect of depression. If you suspect you may be vulnerable to depression, make sure to mention this to your doctor whenever you are prescribed any medications. There is not always a specific cause; if it happens with or without reason, *it is not your fault*. It is the way your brain is wired and a challenge you have to face. Other people have brains wired in different ways and have other challenges. Suffering from depression doesn't make you less of a person. You are a stronger person because you are facing it, and you will conquer it.

Sadness Vs. Depression

Although sadness is an emotion associated with depression, you can be sad without being depressed. If your beloved pet dies, and you cry every night for a couple of weeks but can live your life while still missing your pet, this is normal, and you are sad. However, if you are prone to depression, this could trigger you. Depression is a prolonged experience. It does not necessarily mean you cry every day. What it means is that you are consistently unhappy and will start to lose interest in your life and the activities you used to enjoy. If you are sad, this may happen for a short time, but you will notice it improving over time; with depression, it will get worse. Sadness is a normal, healthy reaction to life events. Depression does not make you abnormal, but it is unhealthy and you need to work hard to overcome it. It will not be easy, but it will be worth it. It may even save your life, and your life is worth saving!

Hopefully, this chapter will never apply to you, and you will never suffer from depression. However, being aware of the symptoms, causes, and outward signs can help you be sensitive to the people around you who may be suffering from depression. Never tell a person suffering from depression to "*Cheer up!*" or "*It's not that bad!*" If they could cheer up, they would. They are not trying to get attention or being overdramatic. For them, it is truly that bad. Instead, ask them if there is anything you can do to help. Remind them that they are a worthwhile person of value. Be there for them. Encourage them to participate in the activities they used to enjoy, but do not attempt to force them. If you suspect they have thoughts of self-harm or suicide, ***tell someone***. Do not wait. Do not worry that they will be mad at you. They might be, but telling someone could save their life.

Do I Have Depression

Ask yourself... Y N

1	Is there a family history of depression?		
2	Have I experienced a recent trauma? If yes, explain. _____		
3	Have I experienced a childhood trauma? If yes, explain. _____		
4	Have I had a recent illness, injury, or begun a new medication? If yes, explain. _____		
5	Have I felt consistently unhappy, sad, or depressed for two or more weeks?		
6	Am I losing interest in my hobbies or activities?		
7	Do I feel worthless?		
8	Do I feel intensely guilty about things beyond my control?		

Ask yourself...   Y   N

9	Do I feel hopeless about my life, or the world in general?		
10	Have I been experienced tiredness beyond what is normal for my level activity?		
11	Have I been sleeping an excessive amount?		
12	Have I been having trouble sleeping?		
13	Have I had drastic changes in my appetite, that are not correlated to changes in my activities or lifestyle?		
14	Have I had increased trouble concentrating?		
15	Have I considered self-harm? (If yes, please immediately reference the beginning of Chapter 6)		
16	Have I had suicidal thoughts? (If yes, please immediately reference the beginning of Chapter 6)		

Ask yourself...   Y   N

***This is not a diagnostic tool. Depression can only be diagnosed by a trained medical professional. Please consider this a tool to facilitate the conversation. Its goal is to help you pinpoint how are feeling, what you are experiencing, and give you a starting point for talking to your parents or guardian, or guidance counselor, or doctor. ***

Managing Depression

There are things that you can do to help yourself get out of mild depression, or as a supplement therapy and medication. None of this should be done in place of the advice of your trained medical professional.

Get moving. When you exercise, your body produces endorphins, which are mood-boosting hormones. When you are feeling depressed, just getting up to exercise can seem like an insurmountable challenge. If you can do it, it is one of the fastest ways to feel better, emotionally and physically. Continued exercise will also have a cumulative effect. It will also help with if you have sleeping problems. It is not a magic pill, but you should notice an overall improvement over time.

Choose your exercise based on your physical abilities. Athletes will not get much of a boost from a short, slow, walk. The same walk could be a great starting point for someone with a more sedentary lifestyle. It is important not to push yourself too hard too quickly. If you get injured, and your mobility is severely limited, you may get even more depressed. For athletes, an injury that forces them suddenly into a sedentary lifestyle can be a trigger for depression.

Reach out. Talk to your friends and family about how you are feeling. Stay connected. People experiencing depression feel they are a burden to their loved ones—this is not true, you are not a burden! People who love you will want to help you. Try to do this face-to-face; it is easier to pretend everything is fine if you are communicating through technology. Your family and friends should know what you are going through so they can help, and understand that if you act differently towards them, it is not personal.

Your friends and family may sympathize and do their best to help, but not be able to emphasize or understand what you are going through, so it can be helpful to **find a local support group**. You will be able to connect with people who are also going through depression, as well as people who have overcome their battle, to help others and to prevent themselves from relapsing into depression. Listen to these people. Use the tools they recommend.

Keep up your schedule of activities and hobbies even if you do not want to. Being in the world and interacting with people will make you feel better than isolating yourself, even if isolating yourself is what you want at the moment. This does not mean that you cannot take time for yourself to be alone and relax, but try your best not to cancel plans so you can wallow in misery instead.

Try to improve your health. Make an effort to get 8 hours of sleep a night. Eat a well-rounded diet, making sure you are getting enough fruits, vegetables, and proteins. Try to eat foods high in B vitamins.[2] B vitamin deficiencies can increase your chances to experience depression. Make sure you are getting enough good fats in your diet, particularly omega-3s.[3] This is a natural mood stabilizer.

Try to get into the sun every day. Even if your depression is not linked to Seasonal Affective Disorder, being in the sun can help. Sunlight increases your body's production of serotonin. Don't forget the SPF! Sunburn never made anyone feel better. If your location or lifestyle does not allow you to get time outside, there are some lamps that mimic the light of the sun, aptly named the HappyLight.

Distract yourself from negative thoughts. You may be told not to think negative thoughts. That is easier said than done. For a depressed person, it may be impossible. When you find yourself spiraling in negative thoughts, do what you can to distract yourself. Watch funny animal videos, play with your pet, read, study, whatever you can do to distract your mind.

---

[2] Most common sources: citrus fruit, leafy greens, eggs, beans, and chicken

[3] Most common sources: fatty fish, like tuna and salmon

Turn off social media, and if you can't, be realistic about what you see. When scrolling through social media posts, it is easy to think that everyone has a perfect life, except for you! It is important to remember that people are posting specific parts of their life for that very purpose, to make themselves and their lives look the way they want them to be. It is important to remember that they are posting exactly and only what they want you to see and are using filters to make everything look even better. They are essentially using marketing strategies to convey messages about their lives. Interpret the images you see in the same way that you would when you see an advertisement online or in print. It very easy to use filters, angles, and apps to appear to have clearer skin, look fitter, thinner, or curvier, living spaces cleaner, vacation locales more impressive, and so on.

Train your mind to think positively. Negative thoughts can be a self-fulfilling prophecy. If you tell yourself you will not be accepted to the college of your dreams, so you don't apply, of course you won't be accepted! Negative thoughts tend to be more automatic than positive thoughts, but with some work, you can train your brain.

Acknowledge the negative thought and analyze it. Is it realistic and rational? Let's revisit our struggling French student. The student has succeeded in getting their grade up to a B but then fails a pop quiz. Their automatic negative thought could be "*I'm going to fail French!*" Realistically, one quiz grade is not going to do significant damage to their grade, as long as it does not become a pattern. If you're five minutes late to your job, you may think, *"I'm going to be fired!"* Really consider this. Is this a first-time offense, or is it a pattern? If you have had warnings, it may be a perfectly rational response. If it is the first time, you could receive a mild reprimand, and that would be the end of it.

Find the facts to prove or disprove your negative thoughts. If you are the first offense tardy employee, check the Employee Handbook for policy on lateness. Have other employees been fired for similar offenses? What have you accomplished or been praised for recently, and does it outweigh this one mistake? What would you say if your favorite coworker asked your advice on a similar situation? Would you tell them they better start getting their desk packed up, or tell them that their boss probably didn't even notice, and if they did, to simply apologize and assure their boss that it won't happen again?

Think "what if" the worst does happen? If the tardy employee gets fired from his position for a minor offense, is that an environment he would want to spend 8 hours a day in? Or would he actually be happier finding a position at a different company? If he is fired, would the world end? Would he spontaneously combust? Of course not. He would go home, vent to his friends and family about his unreasonable boss, work on his résumé, apply for a new job, and begin the process of moving on with his life.

Adjust your original thought. You don't need to be overly positive, just try to *be realistic*. Our tardy employee will come to reassess his automatic "I'm going to be fired!" to "I might receive a warning." You may never become a person whose automatic thoughts are predominantly positive, but you can make them more realistic. This may take a long time, don't be discouraged!

Remember that depression doesn't last forever.
Yes, it's awful; it can be a very difficult time in your life, but it doesn't have to last forever, and you can actively fight it. It will be hard, and it will not happen overnight. But when you have conquered depression, it will be the best feeling! You will notice your automatic thoughts and responses to be more realistic, and hopefully even positive.

Continue to be vigilant. You now have firsthand knowledge of how depression feels, and how you, in particular, think and feel with it. That means if you start to experience the symptoms again, you can start fighting it right away before it really takes hold of your life. The earlier you start, the easier it is. If it does come back, you have not failed. This is simply how you are wired. You fought it before, and you can do it again. ***Never be afraid to ask for help!***

Chapter 7: Self-Confidence Revolution

Self-confidence is extremely important. People often say it is the first thing they notice in a potential romantic partner. It also makes it easier to make friends, and is imperative for the future: college interviews, job interviews, and just dealing with people in general. For some lucky people, self-confidence comes naturally. For others, it is more difficult. The good news is, self-confidence can be learned. Even better, while you are learning self-confidence, you can fake it!

Self-Empowerment

Self-empowerment is the first step to increasing your self-esteem. Everyone has good qualities. Everyone has talents. Although it may feel more natural for many of us to criticize ourselves, it is so much better to empower yourself! Try and think about yourself the way you would talk to your friend. If your friend was feeling worthless because they failed a test, would you tell them they were worthless and stupid? Probably not! Don't tell yourself that either. Be your own friend.

Techniques for Self-Empowerment

Journaling can be a wonderful way to deal with your feelings. However, many teens and young adults don't have much spare time. Pick a journal, notebook app, or agenda, and every day, write three positive things about yourself. This can be difficult. They don't have to be big things. For example:

> 1. I wasn't rude to my mom today, even though she was super annoying.
> 2. My little toe is cute.
> 3. I raised my hand in my worst class today. Even if you don't get called on, give yourself credit for trying!

Listen to yourself and your body. Are you exhausted? Go to bed early. You'll feel better the next day. Are feeling sluggish? Go for a jog. Are you feeling lonely? Reach out to your friend or family member for a chat. Are you feeling overwhelmed and need time alone? Curl up with a book or have a Netflix marathon by yourself. Even though you should not hide from the world habitually, there is nothing wrong with saying no to something and spending time by yourself.

Take care of yourself. The way you present yourself to the world affects how people view you, and the way you feel affects how you present yourself. Personal hygiene is important. If you are on day three without a shower, are you likely to introduce yourself to that interesting new person at school? You don't need the latest fashions, but wear clothes that are clean and neat. Male or female, if you feel better when you wear makeup, take a little time each morning to put it on. However, if you don't like wearing makeup, don't give in to peer pressure to do so. You wouldn't feel confident in it.

Do something to help others. Treating yourself well is great. Helping someone else will make you feel even better. If you love animals, volunteer at the ASPCA. If you love talking about history, volunteer at a nursing home. If you like food, volunteer at a soup kitchen. If you like to work with your hands, volunteer for Habitat for Humanity. There are many worthy organizations, you should be able to find a good fit, no matter where you live. However, you can also do smaller, day to day things. Offer to watch a sibling (for free) when your parents or guardian go out to dinner. Ask that lonely kid who sits alone at lunch to sit with you, but don't act like you are doing them a favor, actually mean it. Hold the door for an elderly person. Give up your seat on public transportation to a pregnant woman. Shovel the snow from your neighbor's sidewalk. Compliment someone. In fact, whenever you're in a social situation and don't know what to say, find something to compliment the person on. It can get the conversation flowing.

Go ahead and fake it. Positive self-esteem cannot be faked. Self-confidence can! It is all about your body language. Tips are discussed in Chapter 2. Mimicking the physical signs of self-confidence can actually make you feel more self-confident.

Positive Affirmation

Positive affirmation is a technique to change your thoughts from negative to positive. These affirmations can often feel awkward and silly, but if you practice regularly, it becomes much more natural. It will help you to feel differently about yourself and improve your life. Basically, you select some goals based on the qualities you want to develop and nurture, what you want to accomplish, and focus on them.

Develop a routine. Pick a couple times a day when you can practice this technique. It can be while you're getting ready for the day or for bed, going for a run or walk, driving (as long as you are still paying attention to the road!) or when you're a passenger in a carpool, bus, etc. Whenever feels right for you. But this is different from meditation, you can multitask, as long that the tasks are mostly physical, and allows you to mentally focus and relax.

Using your affirmations. Before you begin, write down your affirmations. You can use sticky notes and put them where you will see them, or if you want more privacy, use a journal or an app. Affirmations can be thought, spoken, sung, whatever feels right to you.

Sense associations can make affirmations more powerful. For example, use a certain color of a sticky note, pen, or text. With continued practice, you will come to associate that color with your affirmations. Scent can also be a powerful association. This is the sense that is most closely associated with memory in your brain. If you have a favorite perfume or cologne, smell that while you practice your affirmations. Wear this scent on your wrists when you're in situations you may need a self-esteem boost. Take a subtle whiff of your wrist when you need the boost.

Use emotion when practicing your affirmations. Don't use a monotone, even if you are just thinking them. Imbue your affirmations with the feelings you'll experience when you achieve them. Remember as you practice, it is WHEN, not if, you achieve your goal. You WILL get there!

Forgive yourself; don't judge yourself. If you skip your affirmations for a day, or even a week, that's OK. Don't criticize yourself. If you let negative thoughts enter while doing your affirmations, that's ok. Relax, dismiss them, and keep going. If you have trouble getting into the habit, start slow. Pick one affirmation, and one time a day, and build from there as you get more comfortable. Don't be embarrassed. Yes, it feels silly. But you are trying to improve your life and mindset, and that is admirable. Be proud of yourself for even trying.

Examples of Affirmations
- I am confident!
- I like how I look!
- I am learning from my challenges!
- I am good enough!
- I am smart enough!
- I am brave!

- I'm not perfect, and that's fine with me!
- I am kind!
- I belong!
- I am honest!
- My differences make me special!
- I believe in myself!
- I matter!

Setting Goals

One of the best feelings in life are reaching goals. But to reach these goals, you first have to set them. Write them down. Make them as specific as possible. Look at them every day. Use the same app or journal you are using for your self-compliments and affirmations. While goals can be as far-reaching and long-term as you want, it is also important to set small short-term goals. When you reach these goals, you will feel empowered to move on to your bigger goals. If you're artistic (or not artistic but enjoy art anyway) make a dream board. This can be something physical that you hang in your room, or a private Pinterest board. Whatever feels most authentic for you.

Daily Goals

	Goal	Achieved
ex.	Finish homework nightly, not in homeroom the day it is due.	
1		
2		
3		
4		
5		
6		
7		
8		
9		
10		

Short-Term Goals

Goal   Achieved

ex.	Bring up French grade from C to B.	
1		
2		
3		
4		
5		
6		
7		
8		
9		
10		

Long-Term Goals

	Goal	Achieved
ex.	Get into my first-choice college.	
1		
2		
3		
4		
5		
6		
7		
8		
9		
10		

Conclusion

Thank you for making it through to the end of *The Anxiety Workbook for Teens*, let's hope it was informative and able to provide you with all of the tools you need to achieve your goals whatever they may be.

The next step is to get started! Get out there and start practicing, and working on the exercises and challenges provided, and create your own. Embrace and nurture your strengths. Identify your weaknesses and work to overcome them. Never forget that the person you are now is valuable and worthwhile. The intention of this book is not to change you as a person, but to help you grow a happy, healthy, and successful individual, and a productive member of society. While you work towards finding your strength, never be afraid to ask for help. You have more resources than you realize. Knowing when to ask for help shows wisdom, not weakness.

This book should not be used as a replacement for treatment by medical professionals. If you choose to go that route, the information, questions, exercises, and challenges presented here can be used as a tool to recognize issues that you may have and can be used as a starting point for questions you may want to ask.

Be patient with yourself. Your brain and way of perceiving yourself and the world around you was not created in a day. It will take time and effort to adjust. When in doubt, be yourself, but paste a smile on your face and pretend you have confidence. Eventually, the smile will be genuine, and the confidence will not be fake. Be realistic, you don't have to be happy every second of every day to have a happy life. Stay true to you. You are not changing to fit someone else's definition of the right way to be or act. You are growing and will continue to grow throughout your life. Make it the best one possible!

Finally, if you found this book useful in any way, a review on Amazon is always appreciated!

Resources

https://suicidepreventionlifeline.org/chat/

National Suicide Prevention Lifeline, 24 support 1-800-273-8255

https://www.washingtonpost.com/national/health-science/10-nutrients-that-can-lift-your-spirits/2014/01/14/05f4e514-7a4d-11e3-b1c5 739e63e9c9a7_story.html?noredirect=on&utm_term=.9bf65bbe6d24

References

https://www.apa.org/news/press/releases/2014/02/teen-stress.aspx
www.pyschologytoday.com

Our Other Book

Have you noticed that your child is constantly tense all the time? Are they displaying irrational fears occasionally? Moments where they seem to be crippled by fear that it disrupts their daily function? What you could be dealing with is a child with anxiety.

Everyone worries. That is a part of our normal range of human emotion. Even children have worries of their own. But it is when those worries cross over from regular worrying to excessive worrying that starts to disrupt your daily routine that it becomes a problem. Believe it or not, anxiety doesn't just affect adults, but children can be victims of this condition too. **Anxiety is one of the most prevalent disorders in America today**, and it can be challenging for both children and adults who are dealing with this condition. It can also be equally as challenging for the parents, because what can you do to help make it better for your child? How do you protect them from feeling this way?

Anxiety Relief for Kids is a complete workbook which will help your child overcome their worries, stress, anger, depression, panic attacks, and fears with ***proven strategies*** that work.

In this book, you will learn how to:

- Understand anxiety and how it is affecting your child

- Discover anxiety relief strategies and build your own activities toolbox

- How to parent an anxious child

- Engaging games and crafts that you can do to help your child work through their anxiety

- The difference between depression and anger

- What separates panic attacks from fears

The exercises, methods, and strategies which you will uncover in this book will shed light on the importance of helping your child overcome anxiety. More importantly, it is a guide for all parents with anxious children about what *you can do* to help your child through this very challenging emotion that they are dealing with. **All the strategies you have ever wanted to help your child find their happiness again is right here**. They do not have to live a life that is crippled by worries and fears. It is possible to change all that. Improve their self-esteem and help your child find their self-worth once more by freeing them from the grip of anxiety.

This book is packed with all the useful information that every parent with an anxious child needs to help make a real difference in the way that their child deals with anxiety. Overcoming anxiety is going to require practice, time, and effort, and this book will show you just what you need to do to help your child through the process. Put a stop to your child's anxiety once and for all with the *Anxiety Relief for Kids* workbook.

Made in the USA
Middletown, DE
30 September 2019